PIANO / VOCAL SELECTIONS
WITH PIANO RECORDING

RODGERS & HAMMERSTEIN'S™
The Sound of Music™

Music by
Richard Rodgers

Lyrics by
Oscar Hammerstein II

The included CD is playable on any CD player, and is also enhanced so
Mac and PC users can adjust the recording to any tempo or pitch.

ISBN 978-1-4234-9800-1

EXCLUSIVELY DISTRIBUTED BY
HAL•LEONARD®
CORPORATION
7777 W. BLUEMOUND RD. P.O. BOX 13819 MILWAUKEE, WI 53213

Visit Hal Leonard Online at
www.halleonard.com

(Top photo:) Original SOUND OF MUSIC star Mary Martin, flanked by her composer, Richard Rodgers, and lyricist, Oscar Hammerstein II.

(Bottom photo:) Mary Martin and Richard Rodgers listen intently to a "playback" during the album recording sessions for THE SOUND OF MUSIC.

RICHARD RODGERS & OSCAR HAMMERSTEIN

After long and highly distinguished careers with other collaborators, Richard Rodgers (composer) and Oscar Hammerstein II (librettist/lyricist) joined forces to create the most consistently fruitful and successful partnership in the American musical theatre.

Prior to his work with Hammerstein, Richard Rodgers (1902-1979) collaborated with lyricist Lorenz Hart on a series of musical comedies that epitomized the wit and sophistication of Broadway in its heyday. Prolific on Broadway, in London and in Hollywood from the '20s into the early '40s, Rodgers & Hart wrote more than forty shows and film scores. Among their greatest were ON YOUR TOES, BABES IN ARMS, THE BOYS FROM SYRACUSE, I MARRIED AN ANGEL and PAL JOEY.

Throughout the same era Oscar Hammerstein II (1895-1960) brought new life to a moribund artform, the operetta. His collaborations with such preeminent composers as Rudolf Friml, Sigmund Romberg and Vincent Youmans resulted in such operetta classics as THE DESERT SONG, ROSE-MARIE and THE NEW MOON. With Jerome Kern he wrote SHOW BOAT, the 1927 masterpiece that changed the course of modern musical theatre. His last musical before embarking on an exclusive partnership with Richard Rodgers was CARMEN JONES, the highly-acclaimed 1943 all-black revision of Georges Bizet's tragic opera CARMEN.

OKLAHOMA!, the first Rodgers & Hammerstein musical, was also the first of a new genre, the musical play, representing a unique fusion of Rodgers' musical comedy and Hammerstein's operetta. A milestone in the development of the American musical, it also marked the beginning of the most successful partnership in Broadway musical history, and was followed by CAROUSEL, ALLEGRO, SOUTH PACIFIC, THE KING AND I, ME AND JULIET, PIPE DREAM, FLOWER DRUM SONG and THE SOUND OF MUSIC. Rodgers & Hammerstein wrote one musical specifically for the big screen, STATE FAIR, and one for television, CINDERELLA. Collectively, the

United States postage stamp honoring Rodgers and Hammerstein, issued September 21, 1999.

Rodgers & Hammerstein musicals earned 35 Tony Awards, 15 Academy Awards, two Pulitzer Prizes, two Grammy Awards and two Emmy Awards. In 1998 Rodgers & Hammerstein were cited by *Time* Magazine and CBS News as among the 20 most influential artists of the 20th century, and in 1999 they were jointly commemorated on a U.S. postage stamp.

Despite Hammerstein's death in 1960, Rodgers continued to write for the Broadway stage. His first solo entry, NO STRINGS, earned him two Tony Awards for music and lyrics, and was followed by DO I HEAR A WALTZ?, TWO BY TWO, REX and I REMEMBER MAMA. Richard Rodgers died on December 30, 1979, less than eight months after his last musical opened on Broadway. In March of 1990, Broadway's 46th Street Theatre was renamed The Richard Rodgers Theatre in his honor.

At the turn of the 21st century, the Rodgers and Hammerstein legacy continued to flourish, as marked by the enthusiasm that greeted their Centennials in 1995 and 2002.

In 1995, Hammerstein's centennial was celebrated worldwide with commemorative recordings, books, concerts and an award-winning PBS special, "Some Enchanted Evening." The ultimate tribute came the following season, when he had three musicals playing on Broadway simultaneously: SHOW BOAT (1995 Tony Award winner, Best Musical Revival); THE KING AND I (1996 Tony Award winner, Best Musical Revival); and STATE FAIR (1996 Tony Award nominee for Best Score).

In 2002, the Richard Rodgers Centennial was celebrated around the world, with tributes from Tokyo to London, from the Hollywood Bowl to the White House, featuring six new television specials, museum retrospectives, a dozen new ballets, half a dozen books, new recordings and countless concert and stage productions (including three simultaneous revivals on Broadway, matching Hammerstein's feat of six years earlier), giving testament to the enduring popularity of Richard Rodgers and the sound of his music.

*Maria (Mary Martin) and the
Mother Abbess (Patricia Neway)
recall a favorite song they both used
to sing, "My Favorite Things."*

*Maria (Mary Martin) and the
Mother Abbess (Patricia Neway)
recall a favorite song they both used
to sing, "My Favorite Things."*

SYNOPSIS

*This plot synopsis is based on the original stage version.
Differences between it and the 1965 film version are noted.*

THE SOUND OF MUSIC is set in Austria, 1938,
during the rise of the Nazi regime. The story begins
at Nonnberg Abbey, as the nuns are preparing for
evening vespers. Missing among them, however, is a
young postulant named Maria. She has spent the day in
the mountains, basking in the beauty of nature (**"The
Sound of Music"**), oblivious to the fact that she has
stayed beyond the time she was allowed. The sisters are
disturbed by her carefree spirit, and they wonder how to
solve a problem like **"Maria."** They feel she is simply
not suited for the disciplines of being a nun. The wise
Mother Abbess knows that Maria is sincere and devout,
but her natural exuberance is difficult to restrain. When
Maria apologizes profusely for her tardiness (as well
as for singing in the hills), the Mother Abbess gently
prompts Maria to sing a song she has overheard her
singing in the gardens (**"My Favorite Things"**). [*In
the film, this song appears elsewhere.*] Then, to Maria's
dismay, the Mother Abbess instructs her to leave the
abbey for the time being. Her new assignment is to
serve as a temporary governess for the seven children
of a widowed naval Captain. Maria is taken aback by
this daunting task, but nonetheless is willing to obey. As
she departs, she attempts to bolster her confidence with
a reprise of "My Favorite Things." [*The film version
inserts* **"I Have Confidence"** *here instead.*]

Maria arrives at the home of Captain Georg von Trapp
and is startled to find that the household is run in strict
military fashion. His children are dressed in uniforms
and respond to summons from a whistle. The children
expect to chase Maria away within a short time, just
as they have all their previous governesses, but she is
determined to win their trust and affection. Maria soon
discovers that the children know nothing about music,
so she eagerly introduces them to the joys of singing
(**"Do-Re-Mi"**). She later learns from the housekeeper
that, since the Captain's wife died, he has not allowed
any joy—or music—in the household. The children
do not play; they march for exercise instead. Maria,
however, cannot bear to enforce the Captain's rules.

Liesl, the oldest daughter, is sixteen—and of course,
feels that she has no need for a governess to tell her
what to do. She sneaks outside for a rendezvous with her
beau, Rolf Gruber (**"Sixteen Going On Seventeen"**).
Maria catches Liesl sneaking back inside through a
window, but assures her that she has no intention of
telling her father about the incident. A thunderstorm
sends the younger children rushing to Maria's room in
fear, and she entertains them all with a lively song about
"The Lonely Goatherd." [*In the film, this song was
relocated and replaced here by "My Favorite Things."*]

*Mary Martin as
Maria von Trapp*

*"Do-Re-Mi": Maria (Mary Martin)
teaches music fundamentals
to the von Trapp children.*

*During a fierce rainstorm on her first night
at the von Trapp villa, Maria (Mary Martin)
cheers up the frightened children with a
sing-along of "The Lonely Goatherd."*

Captain von Trapp (Theodore Bikel) introduces **5**
Elsa Schraeder (Marion Marlowe) to his children
and their governess, Maria (Mary Martin).

Captain von Trapp invites his fiancée, Baroness Elsa Schraeder, to visit his home. After an extended absence, this is the first time he has returned to his villa since Maria arrived. He is furious when he finds the children playing—worse yet, they are dressed in clothes Maria made from old curtains! He immediately whistles them into a formal line and sends them away to change back into their uniforms. Maria rebukes him for withholding the love his children so desperately long for, but he harshly dismisses her. Suddenly he hears the children singing, and his heart melts. The joy of music he once knew long ago overwhelms him, and he enjoys a much happier reunion with his children. He also begins to see Maria in a whole new light.

The Captain hosts a party in honor of Elsa's visit, but the chatter among the guests eventually turns into a political debate over the Nazis' rumored plans to occupy Austria. As Maria teaches a dance to one of the children, the Captain intervenes and dances with Maria himself. By the time the dance is over, it becomes obvious that feelings have developed between them. The children sing **"So Long, Farewell"** to bid the guests goodnight. Everyone is delighted by this charming adieu—particularly Max Detweiler, who is responsible for finding entertainment for the upcoming Kaltzberg Festival. While Max works to convince von Trapp to allow his children to perform at the festival, Maria—panicked that she might be falling in love with her employer—gathers her belongings and flees from the villa.

Maria returns to the abbey, confused and frightened about her feelings for the Captain in light of her desire to be a nun. The Mother Abbess, however, encourages her to go back to the von Trapp family and face the life and love she has found there (**"Climb Ev'ry Mountain"**). Captain von Trapp and his children are overjoyed by her return, having been quite distraught over her sudden departure. Elsa breaks off her engagement to the Captain following an argument over how they would each face the challenges of the imminent Nazi occupation. With Elsa gone, the romance between von Trapp and Maria develops rapidly (**"An Ordinary Couple"**). [*In the film, this song was replaced by "Something Good."*] Soon Maria and the Captain are married at Nonnberg Abbey (**"Wedding Processional"**).

Meanwhile, the Nazi *Anschluss* (or Annexation) of Austria occurs, with very little resistance. Captain von Trapp, who fervently opposes the German occupation, receives a telegram with explicit orders to report for duty with the Navy of the Third Reich. Refusal is not an option. When the navy Admiral arrives to summon him, Maria buys some time by showing the Admiral the program for the Kaltzberg Festival. The Captain cannot report immediately, she says, because the von Trapp Family Singers are scheduled to perform at the festival in two days. The Admiral agrees to allow the brief respite.

Maria (Mary Martin) and the Captain (Theodore Bikel) dance an Austrian folk step, the "Laendler."

At the festival competition, closely watched by Nazi armed guards, the von Trapp family sings "Do-Re-Mi." The Captain follows with an emotional performance of **"Edelweiss,"** an ode to his beloved homeland. They sing "So Long, Farewell" as an encore, leaving the stage one by one. By the time the soldiers realize what is happening, the entire family has escaped. They flee to the abbey for refuge and hide in the gardens. Rolf Gruber, now part of the Third Reich, is among the soldiers in pursuit, but when he discovers Liesl and the other children, he does not expose them. The Mother Abbess lets the family out through the back gates of the abbey, and they head for the mountains to find their way to safety and freedom.

"Climb Ev'ry Mountain": As the Nuns look on, Maria (Mary Martin) and Captain von Trapp (Theodore Bikel) lead their children over the mountains to safety in the final scene.

As the children and the Nonnberg Abbey Nuns look on, Maria (Mary Martin) marries her Captain (Theodore Bikel).

LET'S START AT THE VERY BEGINNING: THE STORY BEHIND *THE SOUND OF MUSIC*

In 1958 Mary Martin was involved in an exciting new project: the eternally youthful star of SOUTH PACIFIC and PETER PAN, joined by her husband-producer Richard Halliday, had teamed up with the distinguished playwrighting team of Howard Lindsay and Russel Crouse to create a stage play called THE SINGING HEART. It was to be based on a German film, DIE TRAPP FAMILIE, that told the true-life story of the von Trapps, an Austrian family that had fled their homeland following the Nazi *Anschluss* of World War II and found haven in America.

Of course, even in a play Mary Martin would want to sing, so Lindsay & Crouse planned their script to include a sampling of the religious and folk songs the von Trapps had actually sung. Along the way, Martin asked her good friends Richard Rodgers and Oscar Hammerstein II whether they might be willing to write a song especially for her to sing in this new play, just as they had written a ditty, "I Haven't Got a Worry in the World," for Helen Hayes to sing in Anita Loos' 1946 play HAPPY BIRTHDAY.

R&H loved working with Mary Martin. After all, they had produced her sensationally successful National Tour of Irving Berlin's ANNIE GET YOUR GUN, and followed it up by writing what would become her legendary performance in their own SOUTH PACIFIC. But mixing a new song alongside traditional favorites? No thank you. R&H had a better idea: why not let them write an entirely new score for this story—as a musical? That is, if the team already in place would be willing to wait a year since R&H were already working on FLOWER DRUM SONG. The flattering—and wise—decision from Messrs. Martin, Halliday, Lindsay, Crouse and co-producer Leland Hayward: "We'll wait."

The result was THE SOUND OF MUSIC and it represented a challenge for both sets of writers: for Rodgers & Hammerstein, it would mark the only work in their partnership in which Hammerstein's skills were confined to the lyrics only, while Lindsay & Crouse shifted gears from playwrights to musical librettists. However, this quartet enjoyed a warm and fruitful collaboration that was not only pleasant, but speedy: working from L&C's outline, R&H started writing the score in March of 1959. Rehearsals began in August; New Haven hosted the world premiere in October; and Broadway had a new musical hit by November.

Directed by Vincent J. Donehue, with musical numbers staged by Joe Layton, THE SOUND OF MUSIC co-starred Theodore Bikel as Captain von Trapp, Patricia Neway as the Mother Abbess, and Kurt Kaznar as Max. (A year into the run, a newcomer named Jon Voight stepped into the role of Rolf.) With a $5 top ticket price, THE SOUND OF MUSIC boasted an advance sale of over $2 million ($40 million by today's standards).

Original SOUND OF MUSIC star Mary Martin, flanked by her authors: from left to right, composer Richard Rodgers, lyricist Oscar Hammerstein II, and book writers Howard Lindsay and Russel Crouse.

Original sheet music cover

Audiences adored Martin, and took the musical to heart. It ran for 1,443 performances and earned eight Tony Awards, including Best Musical. The original cast album earned a Gold Record and the Grammy Award. In 1961, with the musical still going strong on Broadway, a U.S. National Tour was launched, starring Florence Henderson, and a London production opened at the Palace Theatre, with Jean Bayless and Roger Dann in the lead roles. (Ensconced in the Palace Theatre for more than six years, it held the record for decades as the longest running American musical in London's West End.)

From Broadway, London and "the road," the stage life of THE SOUND OF MUSIC flourished. A perennial favorite in the summerstock, high school, community theatre and regional theatre circuits, it continues to be performed to the tune of over 500 productions a year in the U.S. and Canada alone. Maureen McGovern, Marie Osmond and Shirley Jones are among the stars who led long-running national and international tours. New York City itself hosted several major productions, including City Center (1967), Jones Beach (1970, '71) and New York City Opera (1990); the latter starred Debby Boone as Maria, directed by James Hammerstein.

In 1998 THE SOUND OF MUSIC returned to Broadway in a new production presented by Hallmark, starring Rebecca Luker as Maria and Michael Siberry as the Captain. A Tony Award nominee for Best Musical Revival, its second year on Broadway saw Richard Chamberlain star as the Captain, with Laura Benanti making her starring-role debut as Maria. (Chamberlain subsequently led a successful U.S. National Tour.)

Since the beginning, THE SOUND OF MUSIC has proven to be the most universal of Rodgers & Hammerstein's musicals, and it has played on countless stages all over the world. Between 1996 and 1998 alone, major international productions were presented in Britain, South Africa, Japan, China, the Netherlands, Sweden, Iceland, Finland, Peru, Israel and Greece. In Spring 2004, an American production of THE SOUND OF MUSIC embarked on a tour of the People's Republic of China and southeast Asia, billed as the most extensive tour to date of a Western musical in that region.

And then there is...The Movie. In 1965 the motion picture version of THE SOUND OF MUSIC was released, and made Hollywood history. Directed by Robert Wise, with a score revised by Rodgers (Hammerstein had died in 1960 and so Rodgers composed both music and lyrics for two songs added to the film—"I Have Confidence" and "Something Good"), and a screenplay by Ernest Lehman, THE SOUND OF MUSIC boasted a dream cast: Julie Andrews as Maria, Christopher Plummer as the Captain, Eleanor Parker as Elsa, Peggy Wood as the Mother Abbess and Charmian Carr as Liesl. (Trivia buffs will note that Hollywood's most famous unseen voice, Marni Nixon, here has an on-screen role as Sister Sophia, and that the real-life Maria von Trapp crosses "up screen" of Julie Andrews in a Salzburg plaza during "I Have Confidence.")Winner of five Academy Awards, including Best Picture, THE SOUND OF MUSIC has become the most popular movie musical ever made. From 1965 to 1972 it was All Time Box Office Champ, according to *Variety*. To date it is the highest-ranking musical on the list of top grossing films.

Maria von Trapp (center) greets two of her stage alter-egos from THE SOUND OF MUSIC: Florence Henderson (left), star of the first U.S. National Tour and (right) Mary Martin, Broadway's original Maria.

Following the original release of four years, the film had major U.S. re-releases in 1972 and 1990; it remains popular on the college and revival circuit as well. In August of '96 it was the season finale of the third annual outdoor film festival in New York City's Bryant Park, sponsored by HBO, where it attracted a record crowd of 12,000. In 1998, THE SOUND OF MUSIC was featured in the American Film Institute's roster of the "100 Best American Films of All Time."

The latest and perhaps most unusual chapter in the history of THE SOUND OF MUSIC movie began in England in 1999, when SING-A-LONG SOUND OF MUSIC was born. With the lyrics flashed on the screen, the audience was invited to "sing along" to their favorite songs—all the while dressed in outrageous get-ups inspired by the film (from cross-gender Nun habits to *leiderhosen* and *dirndls*, with high-concept outfits ranging from "whirling dervishes" to "wild geese with moon on their wings").

From a little cinema in London's West End (where it has played twice a week, every week, since August 1999) SING-A-LONG SOUND OF MUSIC soon became a worldwide phenomenon, with showings throughout the UK, Australia and New Zealand as well as Canada, Norway, Sweden, the Netherlands and France.

SING-A-LONG SOUND OF MUSIC reached America's shores in September 2000 with a record-breaking run at New York's Ziegfeld Theater, followed by engagements in Boston, Washington DC, Miami Beach, Chicago, Philadelphia, San Francisco's Castro Theater, Los Angeles' Hollywood Bowl, and elsewhere. SING-A-LONG SOUND OF MUSIC continues to tour America and Europe.

Taking the story full circle, THE SOUND OF MUSIC has emerged as a prime tourist destination to Salzburg, Austria. There in the city where the story is set—and where, in 1964, the movie was filmed—visitors can retrace Maria's steps departing Nonnberg Abbey, sing "Do-Re-Mi" around the same fountains in the Mirabell Gardens and view the exteriors of the two palaces (front and back) that represent the von Trapp villa in the film. This can be done on foot or by taking one of the numerous SOUND OF MUSIC tours that proliferate the city.

More than a hit show or cultural phenomenon, THE SOUND OF MUSIC is a rarity that has touched the hearts of its audiences since the very beginning. Evidently, it meant a great deal to the four men who wrote it, too; Rodgers seemed to speak for them all when, in a letter to Lindsay's wife Dorothy years later, he called THE SOUND OF MUSIC "one of the happiest experiences of my theatrical life."

Maria (Julie Andrews) with the von Trapp children in the Alps

"Bless my homeland forever": On their final night in Salzburg, before their secret escape, the von Trapp Family Singers perform "Edelweiss."

On the set, 1964, posed with the enchanting "Lonely Goatherd" marionettes created by Bil Baird.
From left: Charmian Carr (Liesl), Kym Karath (Gretl), Heather Menzies (Louisa), Angela Cartwright (Brigitta),
Julie Andrews (Maria), Nicholas Hammond (Friedrich), Debbie Turner (Marta) and Duane Chase (Kurt).

Members of the most famous film family in history gather for a reunion 40 years after making THE SOUND OF MUSIC.
Fraulein Maria herself, Julie Andrews (center) is joined by (top row, from left): Charmian Carr (Liesl),
Debbie Turner (Marta), and Kym Karath (Gretl). Front, from left: Nicholas Hammond (Friedrich),
Heather Menzies (Louisa), Angela Cartwright (Brigitta) and Duane Chase (Kurt).
Just "hanging around" behind them are several of the actual Bil Baird marionettes
featured in the film's beloved "Lonely Goatherd" sequence.

CLIMB EV'RY MOUNTAIN

Lyrics by OSCAR HAMMERSTEIN II
Music by RICHARD RODGERS

Maestoso

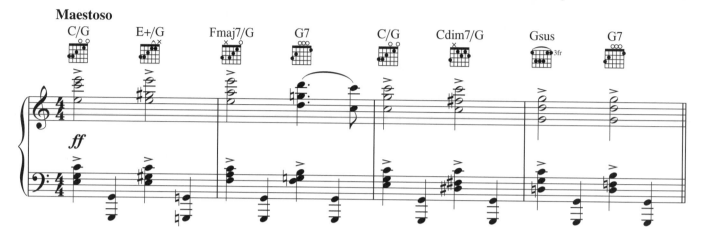

Refrain *(with deep feeling, like a prayer)*

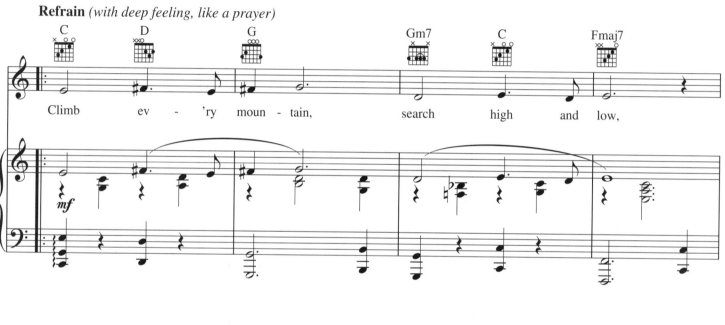

Climb ev - 'ry moun - tain, search high and low,

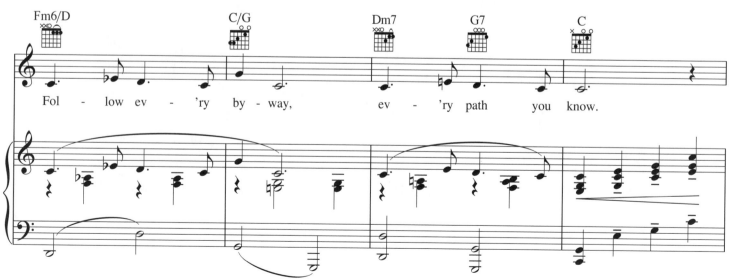

Fol - low ev - 'ry by - way, ev - 'ry path you know.

EDELWEISS

Lyrics by OSCAR HAMMERSTEIN II
Music by RICHARD RODGERS

DO-RE-MI

Lyrics by OSCAR HAMMERSTEIN II
Music by RICHARD RODGERS

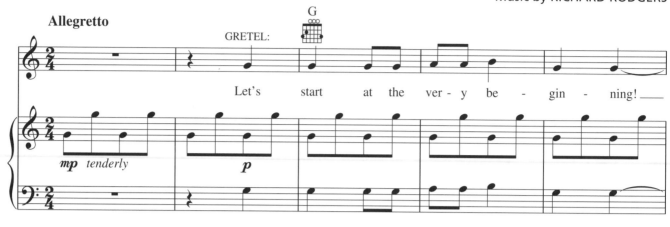

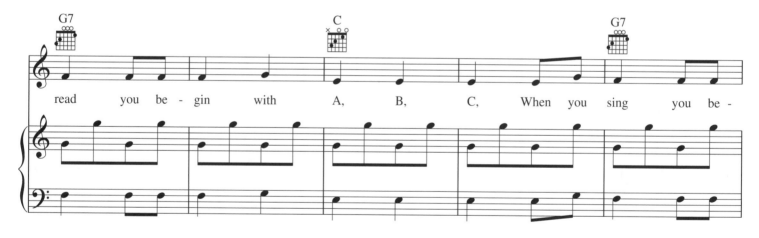

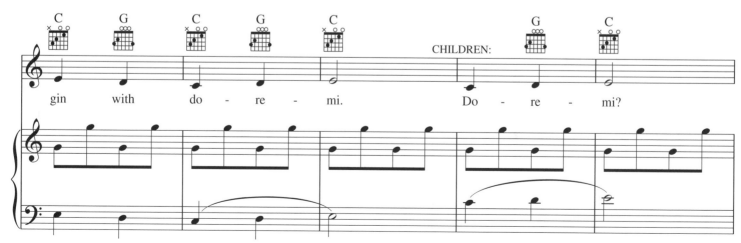

I HAVE CONFIDENCE

Lyrics and Music by
RICHARD RODGERS

Moderato (rubato)

Più mosso

Note: In the film version this song was written to replace the reprise of "My Favorite Things" Maria sings as she leaves the abbey.

THE LONELY GOATHERD

Lyrics by OSCAR HAMMERSTEIN II
Music by RICHARD RODGERS

MARIA

Lyrics by OSCAR HAMMERSTEIN II
Music by RICHARD RODGERS

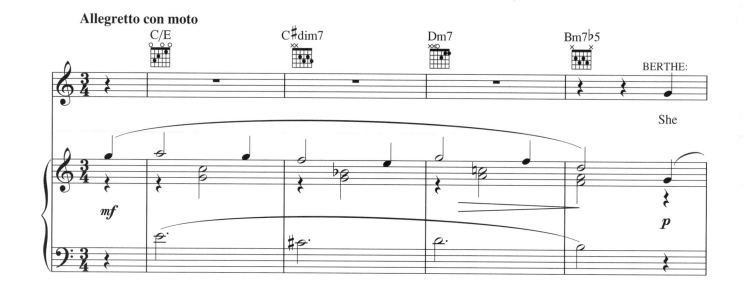

MY FAVORITE THINGS

Lyrics by OSCAR HAMMERSTEIN II
Music by RICHARD RODGERS

When I'm feel - ing sad, _____ I sim - ply re - mem - ber my fa - vor - ite things and then I don't feel so bad. _____

AN ORDINARY COUPLE

Lyrics by OSCAR HAMMERSTEIN II
Music by RICHARD RODGERS

Refrain *(with very warm expression)*

or - di - nar - y cou - ple is

all we'll ev - er be, For

all I want of liv - ing is to

keep you close to me, To

SIXTEEN GOING ON SEVENTEEN

Lyrics by OSCAR HAMMERSTEIN II
Music by RICHARD RODGERS

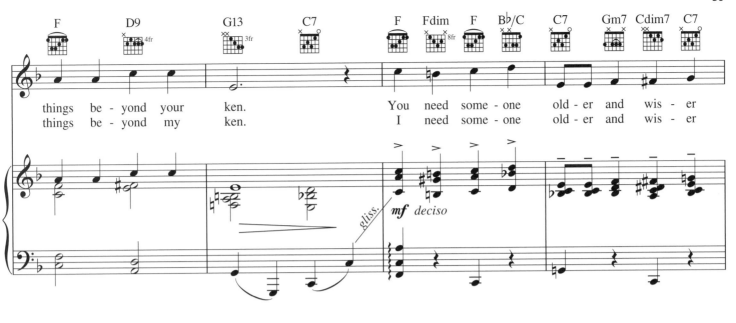

things be - yond your ken.
things be - yond my ken.

You need some - one old - er and wis - er
I need some - one old - er and wis - er

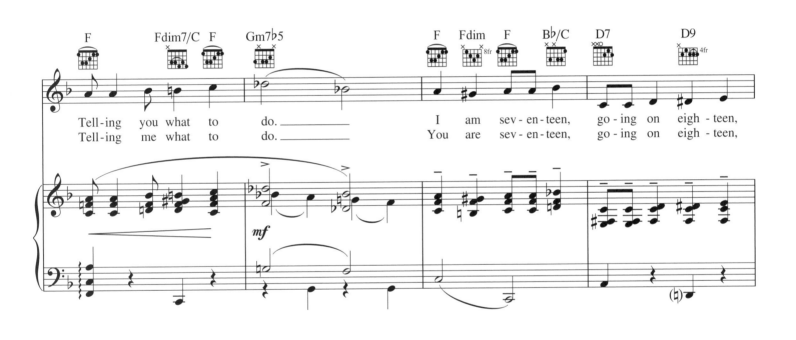

Tell - ing you what to do. _____
Tell - ing me what to do. _____

I am sev - en - teen, go - ing on eigh - teen,
You are sev - en - teen, go - ing on eigh - teen,

I'll ___ take care ___ of you.
I'll ___ de - pend ___ on

Optional ending | *To Interlude and 3rd Refrain*

2

you. _____ you. A

Interlude

bell is no bell till you ring it, A song is no song till you sing it, And

love in your heart was-n't put there to stay, Love is-n't love till you give it a-

SO LONG, FAREWELL

Lyrics by OSCAR HAMMERSTEIN II
Music by RICHARD RODGERS

hate to go and miss this pret-ty sight. ___

CHILDREN:

So long, fare-well, Auf wie-der-sehn, a-dieu, ___ a-

KURT:

dieu, A-dieu, to yieu and yieu and yieu. ___

CHILDREN:

LIESL:

So long, fare - well, Au' - voir, Auf wie - der - sehn, _ I'd

like to stay and taste my first cham - pagne. _

CHILDREN:
FRIEDRICH:

So long, fare - well, Auf wie - der - sehn, good - bye, __ I

leave and heave a sigh and say good - bye, __ good - bye. _____

Meno mosso
Cmaj7

BRIGITTA:
I'm

p legato

LOUISA:

glad to go, I can - not tell a lie. __ I flit, I float, I

SOMETHING GOOD

Lyrics and Music by
RICHARD RODGERS

Note: In the film version, this song replaced "An Ordinary Couple."

THE SOUND OF MUSIC

Lyrics by OSCAR HAMMERSTEIN II
Music by RICHARD RODGERS

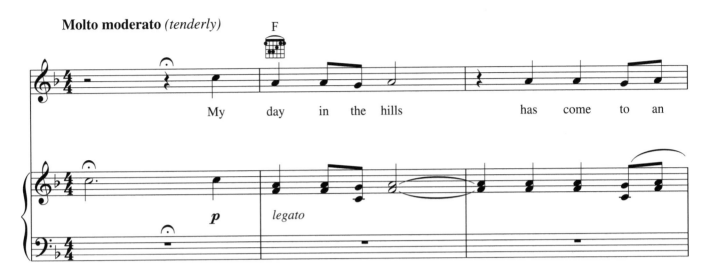

My day in the hills has come to an

end, I know. A star has come out to tell me it's

time to go. But deep in the dark green shad-ows are

WEDDING PROCESSIONAL

Lyrics by OSCAR HAMMERSTEIN II
Music by RICHARD RODGERS

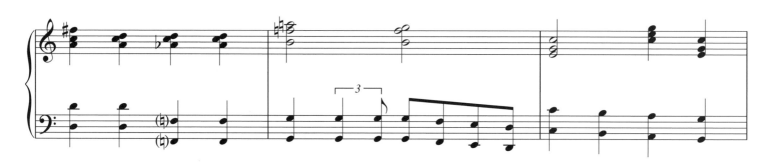

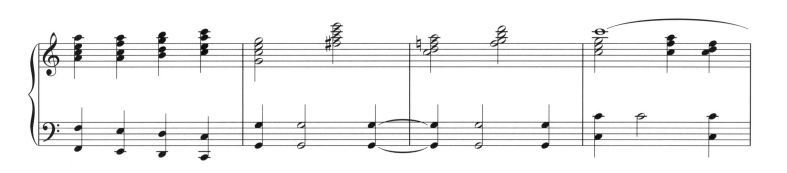

For the entrance of the Bride

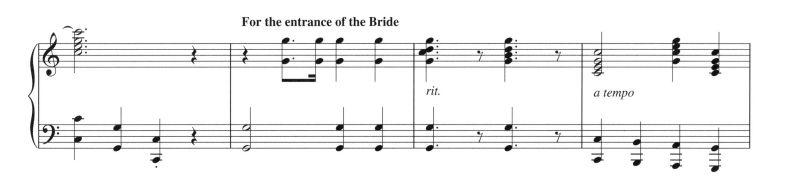

rit.

a tempo

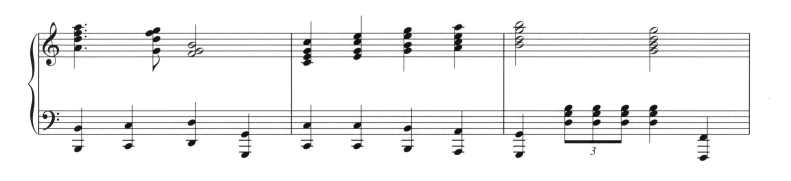